The
Lost
Sun

Also in the **be<u>i</u>ng human** series:

The Flower in the Pocket

The Unwanted Friend

The Dragonfly in the Haze

For more information about the Being Human method, please refer to each book in the series. You will also find a video overview of the method via www.carriehayward.com/beinghuman. Further, you will find more information about the teachings in the list of resources provided at the end of this book.

The Lost Sun

A **being human** guide to
weathering life's storms

DR CARRIE HAYWARD

Illustrated by Elizabeth Szekely

EXISLE
PUBLISHING

First published 2023

Exisle Publishing Pty Ltd
PO Box 864, Chatswood, NSW 2057, Australia
226 High Street, Dunedin, 9016, New Zealand
www.exislepublishing.com

A CiP record for this book is available from the National Library of Australia.

ISBN 978-1-922539-88-5

Designed by Bee Creative
Typeset in Optima, 10.5pt
Printed in China

This book uses paper sourced under ISO 14001 guidelines from well-managed forests and other controlled sources.

10 9 8 7 6 5 4 3 2 1

Disclaimer

While this book is intended as a general information resource and all care has been taken in compiling the contents, neither the author nor the publisher and their distributors can be held responsible for any loss, claim or action that may arise from reliance on the information contained in this book. As each person and situation is unique, it is the responsibility of the reader to consult a qualified professional regarding their personal care.

This book is inspired by an earlier title by the author, *The Woman Who Lost the Sun*. While the essence of the story remains the same, the content and method have evolved in line with the evolution of the Being Human series' concept and purpose.

For Spencer, Alfie and Sullivan,
who make me conscious of
where my attention is, every day.

Dr Carrie Hayward is a clinical psychologist who works with individuals to help them live more consciously and purposefully. Her training in Acceptance and Commitment Therapy (ACT) profoundly changed her approach to living, both professionally and personally.

Introduction

"

How rare and beautiful it truly is, that we exist.

—'Saturn', Sleeping At Last

Being human is truly remarkable. Our mere existence is beautiful, wondrous and mindbogglingly mysterious. But when it comes to the everyday and ordinary experience of being human, at times it can be really hard.

My years as a psychologist have taught me why — that is, the core reason as to why human beings are prone to psychological struggle. I believe this is one of the most important understandings I have learnt about the human condition.

You see, people come to see me, or any psychologist, with a vast range of struggles. Some of us struggle with depressive states or anxiety issues. For others, it may be anger concerns, eating issues, or disharmony in our relationships, and so on. And these experiences are occurring on the background of our own histories and contexts.

It is therefore easy to forget that we are all from the same species, existing together on planet Earth — all trying to navigate life the best way we can. Given our internal world feels deeply private and isolated, we often assume that our psychology is different or abnormal — that there is something wrong with us — which can make us feel alone. Like we do not belong.

Yet despite our differences, all human beings share one of the greatest dilemmas of the human condition: our innate struggle with all the things we cannot control in our lives, including the hardships that happen around us and the emotional pain that happens inside us. And this is underpinned by a core function of our humanness: our survival response. This remarkable aspect of the human condition that keeps us alive can, paradoxically, work against us when we are experiencing hardship and pain. Our hardwired need for control can typically result in a disconnect with ourselves and our core values, which disrupts our way of being with ourselves, each other and the world. And it is when we are disconnected from our values — how we want to show up in the world — that we experience the greatest distress.

In short, our psychological struggle fundamentally occurs when our *humanness* disrupts our *beingness*.

I wrote the Being Human series to explore this dilemma of the human condition. The series is informed by Acceptance and Commitment Therapy (ACT) teachings, an evidence-based framework which helps us to develop psychological flexibility in order to live a mindful, values-based and purposeful life. Put simply, the essence of practising ACT is bringing awareness, and acceptance, to the 'human' in our experience, which allows us to bring choice and meaning to the 'being' in our moments. Allowing us to live our moments, and therefore our lives, as conscious and connected human beings.

"
Life is really simple, but we insist on making it complicated.

—Confucius

The Being Human series features four stories that follow the journey of interconnected characters, illuminating the different ways we experience our shared struggle of the human condition. The stories are followed by an exploration into the teaching and conclude with a practical process for you to take into your life. Each book focuses on a different teaching, and therefore can stand alone, where you will learn one helpful process at a time.

This book in your hands — *The Lost Sun* — focuses on the importance of valued living. Through this story, you will learn how to deal with uncertainty and change through reconnecting to your core values, allowing you to experience meaningful connections with yourself, others and the world.

Each book is one piece of the Being Human puzzle. The whole series — all books connected — forms the complete Being Human method.

By reading about the story of the characters in each book, you may see some of your own experience in their challenges. And hopefully, you will discover the power of awareness around your humanness, allowing you to engage with your values and have choice over your beingness, with yourself, others and the world. This is at the heart of our purpose and meaning as human beings.

And so, welcome aboard to Being Human. I hope you have an insightful and wondrous ride.

x Carrie

The story

Winnie unpacks the final item from her suitcase. She stares at the young woman in the photo. Her heartstrings tug; she can barely recognize herself. Perhaps it's that smile. Or maybe it's the sunshine illuminating her body.

She remembers the day the photo was taken. Jessie had taken it. Almost two decades ago now. It had been a particularly hot summer that year. And seemingly endless. Winnie and Jessie had spent most days lounging in the hot sun in Winnie's backyard; the newspapers and books that were inevitably found in their hands were mere props — too much to say, no time to actually read.

Jessie had always loved this photo, and had once remarked, 'You look as though you are floating above the ground.' It was why Winnie had brought it with her.

Winnie gently places the photo on her bedside table. She catches sight of the freckles on her hand. They are like permanent markings of her hometown, a place where the sun is almost always shining. As a child, Winnie spent most of her spare time outdoors. 'My little sunbeam' her mother would call her. Whether it was capturing caterpillars in old jam jars, making chains of chrysanthemums to crown her head or biting into kumquats snapped off the front garden tree, hoping each one would be less sour than the last. And later in life, daily jogs along the shore of the local inlet, hidden away in a secluded pocket at the edge of town. Winnie has always been drawn to the sun's warm and soothing canopy.

She looks around her now — her new bedroom. In her new apartment. In her new city. These new surroundings are a sharp contrast to her world back home: strangers are everywhere; unfamiliar concrete buildings are wedged together like passengers on a peak-hour train; persistent clouds that barely make room for the sun. Worry grips Winnie's stomach.

Have I made the right decision?

She looks out of her bedroom window. Out there, somewhere, is Jessie. So close to her now. After all this time. Winnie clings to the sliver of excitement that is still there.

She suddenly feels exhausted. She finds her pyjamas and heads to bed. Tiredness manages to trump the worry, and she falls into a long, but shallow, sleep.

The next morning, Winnie wakes to a jittery sensation crawling across her skin. *Watch out*, the goosebumps appear to be warning her. She gets out of bed and opens the bedroom curtains.

The sun has entirely vanished. Ominous, bulging clouds fill the sky. She has never seen the horizon look this sombre. Suddenly the clouds erupt, unleashing a severe downpour.

The noise is thunderous. The wind joins in, blustering the heavy rainfall sideways.

'No!' Winnie gasps, as her body shivers. *How can I go outside in this?* The worry is now peppered with fear and doubt.

She stands numb for a few moments. She compares what she is seeing to the signature skyline of her hometown — a perpetual backdrop of cornflower blue drizzled with the sun's shimmering beams. *And yet I have chosen to leave that behind?* she laments.

Suddenly, impatience knocks in her chest, challenging her to do something. Anything. *I will get rid of the cold.* She races over to the vintage steel radiator in her bedroom and turns it up high. She hurries through the apartment and does the same in every room. Before long, a thick heat begins to percolate throughout all the rooms. It's now sweltering hot.

Winnie collapses on her living-room couch. She is now uncomfortably flushed and sweaty. She trudges back into every room and turns the radiators off.

Winnie then turns her attention to the lights. *I will get rid of the darkness.*

She races around and switches on every light she can find: fluorescent ceiling bulbs, wall lights, floor lamps. The apartment is suddenly lit up like a strobe-light effect at a high-intensity music concert, too glaringly bright.

Winnie begins to feel lightheaded and dizzy. She goes back through each room and switches the lights off.

Desperate to be outside, Winnie fetches two long stem candles and some matches from the kitchen cupboard. She tentatively steps out onto the balcony and places the candles on the concrete beneath her. She lights the candles but the flames woefully falter. The rain and wind unite, swiftly, to dampen them. Extinguishing all hope. Leaving only gloom.

It's no use. She rushes inside and collapses back into bed.

When Winnie wakes the following morning, her first thought is of the sun. She climbs out of bed and walks towards the window, silently pleading that she will find a different sky. But as she pulls open the curtains, it is as though the weather is retaliating. The storm continues; pounding rain and thunderous claps strike through the open window.

She stares at the dark clouds, which appear to permeate the city below — it's hard to see where the sky finishes and the concrete buildings begin. She can't see any brightness. She can't hear any birds. She can't smell the trees.

Watching the people and life outside continuing as normal, Winnie is aghast.

'How can they be out there? Why does nobody care!' She screams at the strangers who cannot hear. She slams down the window and hurls the curtains closed again. It's easier not to see it.

Her wrath is interrupted by a beep coming from the phone on her bedside table. Winnie checks the screen. She sighs and leans over to turn down the volume, ignoring the list of repeated messages asking her where she is. The thought of letting Jessie know she's here brings up an unnerving image of thick roots sprouting from the soles of her feet, and locking her into a life in this colourless and bleak world.

Winnie crawls back into bed. It's comfortable. And it's the closest she can get to a sense of warmth. She falls back asleep.

Time passes and Winnie has lost track of the days. She has continued to hide in bed — her refuge — waiting for the weather to change. As the wind and rain continue to rumble outside, thunderous thoughts circle in Winnie's mind, like intimidating wolves stalking their prey. Worry now leads the pack, fierce and relentless.

What if the sun does not return?

I could never be happy here.

She pulls her bed covers up to her ears, hoping to dampen the noise. But the thoughts and images continue to stalk and are now snarling and harassing her.

What have I done?!

I shouldn't have come here.

Winnie's body joins the torment — her heart is beating heavily, as though it's trying to pummel its way through her chest wall. She rolls over, weightily, on the mattress, attempting to 'steamroll' the discomfort away at the same time. As she does, the photo frame on her bedside table catches her eye. Her kind eyes, open arms and playful smile — an overall aura of calm — appear to be jumping out of the frame, reminding Winnie of how she used to be. She senses a throb deep below her stomach as she remembers how it used to feel. She is longing to feel it. She is yearning to find her 'sunbeam' again.

I need to leave.

I have to go home.

And with that, her pounding heart begins to decelerate, as though it has won the conflict; now having crossed the finish line, it can slow down. Winnie sighs in relief. She feels a different tug deep below her stomach, its protest against her racing chest winning the battle. Winnie ignores this feeling.

Winnie drags her suitcase out from underneath her bed. She opens her wardrobe and begins to remove several piles of clothes, those just recently placed. As her suitcase begins to fill, Winnie feels an ache that has replaced the pounding in her heart. Her stomach tugs at her again. This time it's hard to ignore.

Jessie. Tears start sprouting from Winnie's eyes.

She looks back at the photo frame. An idea springs to mind. Winnie grabs her phone and searches for the nearest post office. She is pleased to see that one is not too far away. She then looks back out the window, inspecting the weather again, and takes a deep breath. *This, I can do*, she coaxes herself, as she takes the photo out of its frame and places it carefully into her pocket, ready to post.

Winnie takes her bright yellow jacket back out of her suitcase. She walks to the cupboard near the front door. All she has from home is her wide-brimmed straw hat and beach umbrella — that's all she's ever needed. She sighs as she grabs them both. It's the best she can do.

When she steps out the front door, the cold air hits and the rain lashes her face. The gusty wind roars at her to stay inside. Her heart hammers in agreement. And a chill, shivering through her body, meddles too. Winnie quickly slams the door closed, shutting out the hostile weather. Her heartbeat slows down.

She then plunges her free hand into her pocket. Her hand falls against the photo. She clutches it tightly and takes a deep breath. Winnie wraps her arms around herself, cradling her body and her beach umbrella in a tight hug, before reopening the front door. Her feet step forward.

She begins walking down the street. Her blood is pumping. Her body starts to thaw. As she turns the corner, she looks up towards the end of the street. Ahead are pockets of various shades of deep green, mixed with scattered specks of orange nestled in amongst the grey backdrop.

'A park!' Winnie exclaims. It's like a feast for her eyes.

She stops walking. She then looks up to the sky — still no sun. But it has at least stopped raining. Winnie takes out her phone to confirm the post office address and then swipes to the virtual map. She discovers that she can detour through the park.

Winnie approaches the park, lined with towering gum trees, and enters. She begins to walk down a crushed gravel pathway. And all of a sudden, a young woman on a bike is riding towards her with accelerating speed. Winnie has no choice but to jump aside, causing her to lose her footing 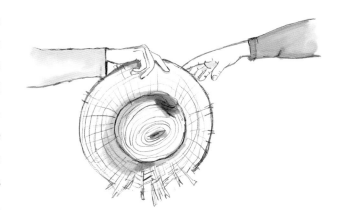 and fall to the ground. The cyclist charges through a deep puddle, showering Winnie with icy water. Shocked and angry, Winnie jumps up, ready to scold this woman who is pedalling away, seemingly oblivious.

But at that moment, a striking bright orange leaf swoops onto Winnie's jacket and interrupts her. The leaf flutters on her sleeve, flaunting its beauty: wedded shades of orange and gold, dappled with scarlet red. With the next gust of wind, Winnie finds herself under a shower of amber leaves, glistening with rain. She pauses for a moment, spellbound. She turns away from the cyclist and starts filling her free pocket with the seasonal leaves.

Winnie continues walking, following the winding path. As she turns a corner, she sees a tall, circular, hedged fence up ahead of her. Situated within the hedge is an old wooden gate. She heads towards it.

Winnie arrives at the old gate, and gives it a push. It swings open easily, with a slight creak. As she walks through, she gasps. In front of her lies a huge, glistening pond — so grand, yet peaceful.

Winnie continues down the gravel pathway, when a sudden gust of wind sweeps the hat from her head. The straw hat begins soaring towards a white peppermint gum tree next to the pond, before catching on one of the tree's branches. A man standing nearby walks over to the tree and reaches up to rescue the hat. Winnie races over. She takes the hat from his outstretched hand, and notices that there is a rip in the hat's brim. Her heart plummets. But she lifts her gaze and smiles at the young man.

'Thank you for your help,' she says, earnestly. He returns the smile.

Winnie secures the hat back on her head, and keeps walking.

An older man is trudging towards her. He looks cold and miserable; out in the cold, wearing no shoes and a shirt that appears to be a pyjama top.

'Please take this.' Winnie slips her beach umbrella into the man's arms as he staggers past her. The man looks at her blankly and keeps moving down the path. Winnie's eyebrows raise in bewilderment. However, she secures her jacket more tightly and continues walking.

The pathway is dappled with puddles of water, still there from the earlier rainstorm. Winnie begins leaping over the puddles, and quickens her pace to see how fast she can go while hurdling each one. The pathway veers to the left, and she has almost made it to the end when she reaches the biggest puddle yet. Winnie stops in her tracks. There is something about the stillness and transparency of this wide, but shallow, puddle that seems inviting. Winnie ponders as she looks down at her shoes. *Well, they are already wet,* she concedes. And before she has a chance to change her mind, she launches both feet off the ground, with each arm swinging in a circular motion by her side, and jumps straight into the middle of the puddle. The water sprays all around her. Winnie then steps forward to the edge of the pond.

She looks down into the water.

She gazes at her reflection. Ripples run across the water's surface.

Winnie looks at the image of her feet. She notices the splotches of mud on her shoes — they are like traces of the bravery that propelled her forward, despite her nerves begging her to stay inside.

Then the ripples dissipate and Winnie can see more clearly. She notices the reflection of the amber leaves spilling from her pocket. Their humble beauty had opened her attention beyond her quick anger at the woman riding the bicycle.

Winnie brings her gaze up to the image of her arms — now empty, but open and free, having given her umbrella to the aloof man sulking through the park.

At the top of her reflection, Winnie sees her hat. It's ripped, but it's back on her head, thanks to the helpful young man. She then lowers her gaze towards the reflection of her eyes; they are etched with a slight gleam as she thinks about her puddle jumping.

There is something familiar about this image in front of her — the playfulness, openness and kindness radiating out of her reflection. The image is without a sun, but there is something else, nestled in amongst the dark clouds, beaming back at her.

It's her smile.

And it feels like the beam of her smile is warming her whole body. She takes a deep breath in, as though she is inhaling her whole reflection. She then takes her phone out of her pocket and types a message:

I'm here. I will see you tonight! x

Winnie turns away from the pond and begins to head through the park, the same way she came. She will go back 'home' to unpack her suitcase once again.

Afterword

Suffering in the storm

At times, life will go wrong for all of us. Bad weather inevitably comes our way. And when it does, we naturally experience emotional and/or physical discomfort. How we are feeling at any given time — including how happy we feel with what is happening in our lives — is therefore not guaranteed. This is part of being human and living in a changeable and unpredictable world.

The problem is that the mind interprets normal but uncomfortable emotional pain as signals of a threat that must be resolved. This is due to our survival response — the response that prepares the body with physiological changes to react to danger. This adaptive function was necessary for our primitive ancestors, who had to react quickly to external threats to stay alive.

Accordingly, the mind deems that we are *safe* only in the absence of emotional pain. The mind's primary job is therefore to attempt to control or prevent anything that might go wrong; it desperately seeks control of the outside world to ensure comfort within us.

Given this need for control, our minds are typically intolerant of unknown or uncertain situations and environments. Again, this intolerance has an evolutionary foundation — unfamiliar and unpredictable situations made it difficult for our ancestors to prepare for, and potentially defend against, potential threats (e.g. dangerous predators, dire weather, etc.) in order to stay alive. The mind therefore feels safer by either avoiding unfamiliar experiences, and/or preparing for the unknown by engaging in unhelpful thinking patterns. This includes 'what-if' thinking and playing out the worse-case scenario (also called 'catastrophizing') in our heads. The mind is trying to find control any way it can.

A further side effect of our hardwired survival response and need for control is that we are regularly evaluating the 'goodness' of our lives based on what is going on around us or inside of us. The mind operates through a doctrine of 'I will be okay only if everything around me and inside of me is okay'. Which is why for many of us, the illusion of a 'good' or 'happy' life is dependent on life going well, and therefore on us feeling good.

In the story, Winnie's initial reactions to the unwanted weather and her internal discomfort illustrate our mind's instinctive reactions. Her attention was stolen by external events. Her behaviour was consumed by trying to seek comfort within. But these reactions only made Winnie feel worse. For two reasons: not only did she continue to experience discomfort about the uncontrollable weather, but her attempts to control it (including avoidance and catastrophizing) disconnected her from the person she used to be and the person she wanted to be again.

This hardwired need to control pain can therefore cause us further distress, often underpinning our experiences of anxiety, anger and despair. When we are not aware, these internal reactions can trigger us to engage in behaviours that further increase our pain. And it is when our behaviours and attention are disconnected from the person we want to be, that we experience the greatest suffering of all.

Finding sunshine in the storm

Despite our mind's conviction, we cannot control the 'weather'. Life will go wrong and will cause us pain, beyond our full control. But how much we suffer with pain, and how connected we remain to ourselves and our life's meaning and purpose, is determined by how much we make room for discomfort and how we show up in the storm.

It ultimately comes down to the conscious awareness of ourselves. That is, how mindful we are of our internal reactions (our humanness) and how we choose to respond with, and attend to, our core values.

Values: our scaffolds and our stars

Our core values echo who we are at heart. They are the qualities we want to stand for while we are alive, and what we want to be remembered for after we are gone. In essence, our core values are how we ideally want to behave as a human being.

Being mindful of, and choosing, how we want to behave as human beings — towards ourselves, others and the world around us — brings meaning to our moments and purpose to our lives.

Winnie began to reconnect to her values — being playful, kind, open and calm — once she stepped through her front door and into the world. As Winnie became more connected to herself and her surroundings, her suffering began to lessen, even with the discomfort of the unwanted weather still there.

When Winnie eventually found her smile, it was not because she had found the 'sunshine' around her. And it was not because she necessarily felt comfortable or 'happy' inside. But rather, Winnie had found her smile because she saw, in her reflection, that she had reconnected to her core values. In the very simple moments and humble interactions with others and the world, Winnie saw herself behaving with playfulness, kindness and openness. And this gave her security, purpose and meaning in moving forward with the unknown and unfamiliar change in her life.

Values function as both our *scaffolds* and our *stars*. They are our *scaffolds* by helping us deal with life going wrong, and by helping us find security and meaning in how we show up in what we are dealing with. Whether it be daily stressors, difficult interactions with others, or the bigger tragedies that we experience in life, knowing that we can always choose to respond consciously and consistently with our values keeps us grounded and secure within ourselves. This, in turn, grounds us in a world that we cannot control, and helps us move in a purposeful and meaningful direction, even when life is causing us pain.

Moreover, values function by shining a *starring* light on our daily moments — by bringing attention to what we care about and who we choose to be. This brings awareness and meaning to our everyday moments — which can turn our ordinary moments into something extraordinary.

In summary

Our psychology is hardwired to keep us safe by trying to find comfort and control in a world that we cannot control. This includes what is happening around us, and what is happening inside of us. Our need for control can regularly cause us to move away from our values, creating psychological suffering.

However, we can be aware of this human tendency. We can normalise this tendency, which allows us to have self-compassion. And rather than allowing our mind to demand certainty and trust from the world, we can instead trust *ourselves* by connecting to our core values through our behaviours. Instead of craving external control, we can focus on how we *behave* in the external world. And instead of needing to feel comfortable, we can gently make room for discomfort and attend to the *value* in our actions and our way of being.

We can simply ask ourselves one very basic but powerful question:

Who do I want to **be** in the world right now?

This simple question gives us access to our values. We can then make a choice to attend to and live our values in our behaviour in that very moment, regardless of what is happening around us or inside.

If our attention is on living our core values, then we can show our mind that control and comfort are not required to feel secure, purposeful and empowered. We can see the good life to be one of 'meaning' rather than one of 'happy'. And we can find our sunbeam, even when it is raining outside.

The Being Human method

The Being Human method brings together each process presented in the four books of the Being Human series. It is a method that involves four steps for awareness and connection. The first two steps — 'hello mind' and 'hello heart' — allow us to be aware of our humanness. The second two steps — 'hello being' and 'hello world' — allow us to connect to our beingness with ourselves, our fellow humans and the physical world.

You can practise just one step or the full method, in any moment. It is particularly helpful when you are experiencing psychological distress or unhelpful distraction/ disconnection.

1. Hello mind

a. Notice your thoughts — that is, what your mind is saying to you.

b. Identify whether these thoughts are a familiar 'story' that your mind has told you before. For example, your mind might be telling you thoughts around the 'I'm not good enough' story or the 'No one cares about me' story.

c. Ask yourself whether your thoughts are helping you right now.

'Hello mind. These thoughts are an old story.
They are not helping me right now.'

2. Hello heart

a. Name the feeling/sensations in your body.

b. Identify the value underneath the feeling — what is it that matters to you for this feeling to be there?

c. Allow the feeling/sensations to be there (without judging yourself or the feeling).

It can help to ground yourself by placing a hand on your heart and taking a slow, deep breath as you gently say to yourself:

> *'Hello heart. I am feeling [...]*
> *because I care about [value].*
> *And that's okay.'*

And now that you are connected to your values ...

3. Hello being

Say hello to who you want to be in the world.

    a. Check in with your values (i.e. the person you want to be) in that moment.

    b. Choose a response/behaviour in alignment with your values.

Gently say to yourself:

> *'Hello being. Who do I want to be in the world right now?'*

4. Hello world

Say hello to the world around you. Reconnect to the physical world, including nature and people around you, by connecting with your senses.

Don't just see, but watch.

Don't just hear, but listen.

Don't just touch, but feel.

Don't just smell, but inhale.

Don't just taste, but savour.

And where appropriate, bring a 'wow' to that experience.

'Hello mind. Hello heart.
Hello being. Hello world.'

Resources

General resources

Baird, J. 2020, *Phosphorescence: On awe, wonder and things that sustain you when the world goes dark*, 4th Estate.

Brown, B. 2021, *Daring Greatly: How the courage to be vulnerable transforms the way we live, love, parent, and lead,* Penguin Life.

Carlson, R. 2017, *The Sense of Wonder: A celebration of nature for parents and children*, HarperCollins Publishers.

Coates, K. and Kolkka, S. 2022, *How to Be Well: A handbook for women*, Simon & Schuster.

Goodwin, K. 2023, *Dear Digital, We Need to Talk*: *A guilt-free guide to taming your tech habits and thriving in a distracted world*, Major Street Publishing.

Hari, J. 2022, *Stolen Focus: Why you can't pay attention*. Bloomsbury.

Johnson, S. 1999, *Who Moved My Cheese? An amazing way to deal with work and your life*, Vermilion.

Katie, B. 2018, *A Mind at Home with Itself: How asking four questions can free your mind, open your heart, and turn your world*, HarperOne.

Siegel, D. J. 2016, *Mind: A journey to the heart of being human*, W.W. Norton & Company.

Siegel, D, J. 2012, *Mindsight: The new science of personal transformation*, Bantam Books.

ACT resources

Eifert, G.H., McKay, M. and Forsyth, J.P. 2006, *ACT on Life Not on Anger: The new Acceptance & Commitment Therapy guide to problem anger*, New Harbinger Publications.

Harris, R. 2016, *The Single Most Powerful Technique for Extreme Fusion*, e-book, www.actmindfully.com.au/upimages/The_Single_Most_Powerful_Technique_for_Extreme_Fusion_-_Russ_Harris_-_October_2016.pdf

Harris, R. 2021, *The Happiness Trap: Stop struggling, start living*, 2nd edition. Exisle Publishing.

Hayes, L.L., Ciarrochi, J.V. and Bailey, A. 2022, *What Makes You Stronger: How to thrive in the face of change and uncertainty using Acceptance and Commitment Therapy*, New Harbinger.

Hayes, S. 2019, *A Liberated Mind: How to pivot toward what matters*, Avery.

Hayes, S.C. and Smith, S. 2005, *Get Out of Your Mind and Into Your Life: The new Acceptance and Commitment Therapy*, New Harbinger.

Leonard-Curtain, A. and Leonard-Curtain, T. 2019, *The power of small: How to make tiny but powerful changes when everything feels too much*, Hachette.

LeJeune, J. 'Pain and value: Two sides of the same coin', https://portlandpsychotherapy.com/2012/06/pain-and-values-two-sides-same-coin-0/

Oliver, J., Hill, J. and Morris, E. 2015, *Activate Your Life: Using acceptance and mindfulness to build a life that is rich, fulfilling and fun*, Constable & Robinson.

Acknowledgments

A heartfelt thank you to the team at Exisle Publishing for giving these books a welcoming home. A particular thank you to Gareth for seeing the potential in this series and to Anouska, Karen and Enni for taking such good care of these stories.

To the very talented Lizzie Szekely — I adore working with you and am constantly dazzled by your creative mind and your beautiful illustrations. Thank you for being so dedicated to these books and for befriending the 'W' characters the way you have.

I would like to thank Virginia Lloyd for her brilliance in editing the earlier versions of this series, and for her overall support in shaping this vision.

There were a number of friends and colleagues who generously gave their time to read initial manuscripts in this series and give their feedback: Kate James, Russ Harris, Aisling Curtain, Louise Hayes. I would also like to thank other folk within the ACBS community, for introducing me to ACT and for creating such a supportive community.

I am hugely grateful for my friends and family:

Warwick — for being a loyal cheerleader of this series. And of us.

Amber and Trinity — for your enthusiasm and support.

Ryan — for the time, care and wisdom you have given this series. Your way with the written word blows my mind.

My parents — Mum, Andrew, Dad and Chrissi — for your endless love, support, and for your devotion to your grandchildren.

Spencer, Alfie and Sullivan — you are my best little teachers of being attentive, curious and playful.

Thank you to all the human beings who have joined me in my therapy room — thank you for trusting me. Thank you for teaching me.

And finally, thank you to everyone who stepped into the first version of Winnie's world, and to those embarking on this Being Human series. I hope that reading the characters' stories helps you to normalise and choose compassion for our complex humanness, and to revel in our extraordinary world.

It really is so rare and beautiful that we even exist.